The Norwegian Jakt Stine Katrine

The people around her
and
the machinery within her

George Edwards

Fleeton Wharf Forlag

Reedville, VA

ISBN 978-0-5789-8197-0

Table of Contents

Introduction

For me, this project began at Mystic Seaport in Connecticut. On display at the Seaport is a massive two-cylinder engine which had been built in Norway and whenever I visited the Seaport, I would stop and stare and try to understand how it worked. However, the display did not provide a history of which vessels the engine might have been in. How did this large, heavy item from Norway end up in Connecticut? In 2013, I decided to dig in and learn the story behind the engine, and with a challenge like this, I can become quite determined. On the Seaport Museum's website, the entry about the engine gave the name of the vessel, *Anne Kristine*, but claimed the engine was installed in 1910, which turned out to be far off. Correspondence with the museum provided one more clue; *Anne Kristine* had two masts. Online searches for 'schooner Anne Kristine' slowly uncovered some leads. There were some false leads. The jakt *Anna Kristina* (now named *Dyrafjeld*) was active in Norway and it took a while to rule her out. (There is a very nice book on her by Toril Grande and Anders Slembe. See the list of references.)

What started as some basic research on the engine grew into an extensive research project on the vessel which the engine had once driven as well as research into other engines in her past. I had already acquired a good grasp of the Norwegian language which made the research possible.

One of my inquiries went to a former owner in Norway and fortunately he forwarded it to Tolleif Hidle on Bømlo. It turned out that Tolleif knew *Anne Kristine* since he was 13 years old and he was working to "nøste opp" [1] her history. We started a collaboration and friendship which lasted for three years and would have continued except that Tolleif passed away in May of 2017.

---

[1] Gather up, literally wind yarn into a ball

Tolleif knew, and made contact with, many people who helped us with the story:

> Oddvar Vinje – He knows everything about Hardanger jakts and their owners at Jondal and is a talented model maker.

> Jan Willy Folgerø-Holm – He is a former Wichmann employee who dug through the files at the Wichmann archives and who provided a connection to Sindre Nilsen who finally cracked the mystery of the engine's history.

> Kjellaug Arnulf – She was the communication link between Tolleif and Norman Baker.

> Oddny Barmen – She is a descendent of the first owner and was very helpful with their family history. Oddny provided a connection to Tracy Higgins in the U.S. who helped and provided a family picture.

> Göran Grauers – He is an owner from Sweden who provided an expansive manuscript on his experiences.

> Norman Baker – An American, he was the final owner. He corresponded with us and provided drawings of *Anne Kristine* and a film documentary of his experiences.

I am grateful for all their support and cooperation.

On a visit to Norway in October of 2017, I received a warm welcome from Tolleif's family and friends. There I saw the original shop where the Wichmann concern once operated and a collection of their vintage engines. I visited Halsnøy where the vessel had been built and Jondal which was once her home port; then on to Norheimsund where I saw the restored jakt *Mathilde*. Ironically, when I visited The Norwegian Maritime Museum in Oslo in 2012, I got a good look at the jakt *Gjøa*, but at that point I didn't know that I would be researching a jakt.

I will use the pronoun "we" a lot to include Tolleif in the process since, in many ways, this started out as his project.

The first incarnation

This is the story of a vessel, of a type called jakt, that was afloat and in service for 123 years. Such a long life is exceptional. While some vessels have been around this long, they have spent years idle at a pier or on solid ground. *Gjøa*, the jakt that Amundsen sailed and motored though the Northwest Passage, is, in 2021, 148 years old but has been on land for 111 yrs. The jakt *Mathilde* is now afloat and in great shape after a major rebuild but was built 16 years after the vessel in our story.

Our vessel has had three names. She was named *Stine Cathrine* when finished in 1868, *Åsta 1* in 1935, and *Anne Kristine* in 1952, a name she kept through four owners over 39 years. While *Stine Cathrine* was the vessel's official name, she was more often referred to as *Stine Katrine*, which is pronounced the same as *Stine Cathrine* [2]in Norwegian. She was a working vessel that even in the last years had to earn a living doing charters.

The jakt *Stine Katrine* was named for a young girl who lived at Hetland near Innbjoa on the Bjoafjord (Bjoafjord connects the Hardangerfjord with the Skånevikfjord). Stine was 14 years old when the jakt was built in 1868 and she was confirmed in the church in the fall of the same year, a very important step in that society.

Let's step back and start the story with Stine's grandfather, Sten (Steen) Ellingsen Hetland who was born in 1791. We know that in 1834 he had the jakt *Forsøget* (The Attempt) built. She was built by Henrich E. Nachschow at Koven på Sjo on Halsnøy. She was 43 n. feet [3] on deck and 16 n. feet wide.

---

[2] In Norwegian every syllable is pronounced and vowel sounds are shifted from English. Thus, Anne Kristine is pronounced Ah-neh Kris-tee-neh; Stine Katrine – Stee-neh Kah-tree-neh

[3] n. feet = Norwegian feet which are slightly longer than English feet.

Unfortunately, "Forsøget" is a very common name so it is hard to trace the vessel's history.

Sten had several children. His son Johannes took over the estate when Sten died in 1840 but then Johannes drowned in 1846. The next oldest brother, Elling (born 1824), took over the estate at that point. Elling Stensen Hetland married Anne Karine Johannesdatter Håvarstein and their first child, Stine Katrine, was born in 1854. She was originally named Stene or Stena for her grandfather and Katrine for her grandmother. Elling and Anne Karine also had three sons; Sten, Elling and Anton. Anne Karine died in December of 1861 and Elling remarried.

Elling Stensen Hetland

Elling was a farmer, merchant and vessel owner. He operated a general store and a barrel factory at Innbjoa. He was one of the first from the Bjoa area to pursue trading in fish in Lofoten and farther north (reference Tvedt). In the klippfisk trade they would buy skrei[4] cod on the fishing grounds in the Lofotens, dress and salt them then bring them back to Innbjoa to dry them on the rocks. Most operators dried their fish closer to the fishing grounds, particularly in Kristiansund, but that could get quite crowded. On the trip north they would carry salt, barrels, and other cargo. The herring fisheries were a good complement to the cod fisheries and that took place in local waters as well as in northern locations.

Elling was an important member of the community and on a least one occasion served in district court on a small panel of jurors as a lagrettemann. This was during the fall circuit court for Fjeldbergs Thinglag in 1857 where he and three others served under Mons Lie the sorenskriver, or circuit judge. Mons Lie was the father of Jonas Lie, the author [5].

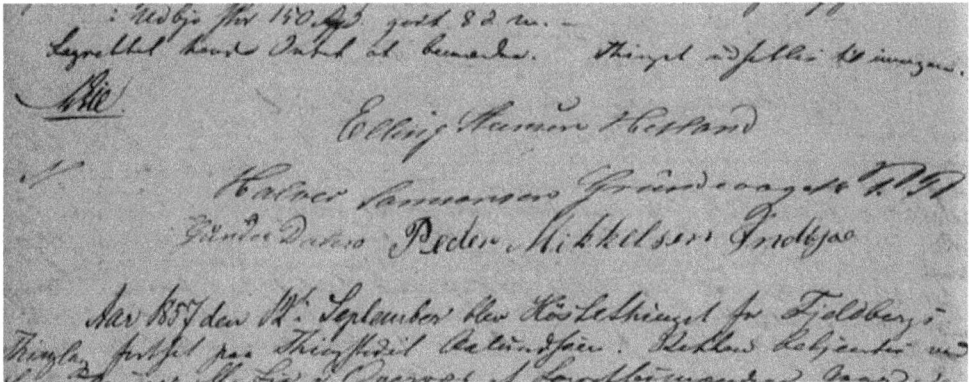

A clip from the "tingbok" showing signatures at the end of the first session and the text of the beginning of the second session. The signature of Mons Lie appears in the upper left corner and Elling's signature is in the upper middle.

---

[4] Skrei - mature cod that migrate to the Lofotens to spawn.

[5] Jonas Lie was a novelist, poet, and playwright and was ranked with Ibsen, Bjørnson, and Kielland.

The jakt *Anne Karine* was built in 1857, apparently as a partnership of Elling Hetland and Sjur E. Hetland who was listed as the principal owner. That Elling was a major partner is evident in that the vessel was named for his wife. Sjur E. Hetland appears to be the son of Sjur Johannesen and Gertrud Eriksdatter Hetland. Sjur Johannesen died before Sjur the younger was born and it appears that the son took his mother's surname. He was only 18 years old when *Anne Karine* was built. Perhaps he had a significant inheritance from his father. By 1864 the ownership of *Anne Karine* had changed to Petter von Tangen and Elling Hetland, and by 1869 she was owned solely by von Tangen. There appears to be a long-standing business relationship with the merchant von Tangen who had his office and warehouses in Bergen. His story appears below.

Anne Karine was built at Innbjoa by a traveling shipbuilder named Gjert Andersen Eide probably using timber from the Hetland property. She traded regularly to the Baltic as well as Lofoten and Nordland.

It is quite fortunate that there is a painting of *Anne Karine* in the Bergen Maritime Museum. It was painted by Fredrik Sørvig [6] in 1865 when she was owned by Hetland and von Tangen, and it probably hung in von Tangen's office. The color scheme is seen in other jakt portraits and may be that of von Tangen's fleet. Her skipper at this point was Ole K. Flage. The portrait of *Anne Karine* may be as close as we can get to what *Stine Katrine* originally looked like since we have not found pictures of her.

---

[6] Fredrik Martin Sørvig was a very prolific painter of ship's portraits and the clear choice for ship owners in Bergen. There are 81 of his works in the Bergen Maritime Museum alone.

Portrait of *Anne Karine* by Fredrik Sørvig
courtesy of the Bergen Maritime Museum

Notes on *Anne Karine* from a listing of paintings in the museum.

In 1868, Hetland arranged to have another jakt built by Gjert Eide. This time it was built on Halsnøy and would be named ***Stine Katrine***, our main subject. This was a hectic time for jakt building. Dozens were built in 1868 just in Sunnhordland (the southern section of Hordaland County).

Next, Hetland bought the jakt ***Fremad*** which had been built just east of Innbjoa at Vake in 1869. In this time period, the practice was for the building master and his main helper to come before the circuit court to witness that they had built a vessel and to describe its size and construction. A copy of this was required for foreign trade to prove that the vessel was Norwegian. The document was called a bilbrev[7] and corresponds to a carpenter's certificate in the United States. Bilbrevs, as recorded in court records, form a valuable source of data on Norwegian vessels. The curious thing here is that Thrond Halvorsen Vake who gave witness in court as the building master for ***Fremad***, was only 18 years old and listed as "løskar", which means having no fixed occupation.

---

[7] Bilbrev – A document attesting to the origin of a vessel. Literally "axe-letter" from "biil", an old word for axe.

12

There must have been a skilled building master on site but why he didn't testify isn't known.

For *Stine Katrine* the building master and his helper did appear in court. Below is my translation of the bilbrev for *Stine Katrine*.

September 14, 1868

Carpenter's certificate testimony

Gjert Andersen Eide, farmer, 45 years old, and Tørris Andersen, lower Tofte, farmer, 32 years old, came forward and testified that in the current year in Fjelberg Parish S.B.A. (Southern Bergenhus County) the Kingdom of Norway have the first as builder and the other as assistant, built a jakt vessel which is given the name Stine Katrine, that its building method is carvel, that all materials are Norwegian, consisting of pine, with the exception of that for the stern post, lot*, windlass bitts and some other small items is utilized oak, that the vessel has a length of keel 25 Al 8 Tom, between the stern post and stem 31 Al 18 Tom, breadth at the mast 9 Al 18 Tom and depth at the mast 3 Al 21 Tom, all approximate. This testimony they confirmed by oath.

*The 'lot' is an extension of the keel which connects to the stem.
Al = alen = 2 Norwegian feet, Tom = inches

The table below lists the jakts owned by the Hetland family at different times. Dimensions are in Norwegian feet (f) and inches (t).

Anne Karine and *Stine Katrine* were of similar size while *Fremad* was smaller.

Year	Name	Length on deck	Beam	Depth	Draft	Owner	Builder
1834	Forsørget	43 f.	32 f.	16 f.	3 f.	Steen E. Hetland	Nachschow
1857	Anne Karine	65 f. 5 t.	50 f.	18 f. 11 t.	8 f. 3 t.	Sjur E. Hetland and E. S. Hetland	Eide
1868	Stine Katrine	63 f. 6 t.	50 f. 8 t,	19 f. 6 t.	7 f. 9 t.	Elling Stensen Hetland	Eide
1869	Fremad	52 f. 4 t.	40 f.	17 f. 7 t.	6 f. 9 t.	Elling Stensen Hetland	unknown

Features of a Jakt

Fore and aft rig with a main, topsail, three foresails and a square sail that could be set for downwind sailing.

Bow sprit and jib boom.

Tall mainmast in one piece. No topmast.

Transom stern.

Rudder hung on the outside. A short tiller controlled by tackle.

Crew quarters forward, hold amidships Skippers cabin aft.

Large jakts were sometimes converted to a ketch rig, the rig of a Galeas.

The word jakt is related to yacht, from the dutch, and originally meant a fast sailer. Jakt first applied to the rig but later came to apply to the rig and the hull.

Gjert Andersen Eide (1820-1901)

Gjert was one of several traveling shipbuilders from Halsnøy and one of a group called the Halsnøy-Masters (Reference Nerhus). In the mid-1800s shipbuilders would often build vessels in locations suited to the buyer. Perhaps the buyer had timber nearby or a source of labor. Since everything was done with hand tools there was not much required for a building site other than a plot of land that sloped into the sea. Gjert built at Innbjoa, Opsanger, Røssland, Undarheim and on Halsnøy. He married the daughter of Henrich Nachschow who was a well-respected shipbuilder of the previous generation. Gjert probably learned the trade under Nachschow at Koven på Sjo on Halsnøy and later built vessels there himself. Gjert also worked with Per Hagen, Nachschow's son and Gjert's brother in-law. Gjert had a farm at Eidsvik on Halsnøy.

The table below lists boats known to be built by Gjert but it probably isn't comprehensive. The first seven are from a list in <u>Frå Vikings Tid til Vår Tid</u> by Nerhus. Dimensions are in Norwegian feet (f) and inches (t).

Year	Location	Type	Name	Length on deck	Beam	Depth	Draft	Owners
1855	Opsanger	jakt	Emma	50 f. 6 t.	40 f. 3 t.	17 f.	7 f. 2 t.	Lars K., Knut L. & Brynjulf L. Opsanger
1856	"	jakt	Frigga	68 f. 2 t.	54 f.	19 f.	8 f. 5 t.	Axel & Wilhelm Undahl
1856	"	jakt	Allegro	63 f. 2 t	50 f.	18 f.	7 f. 10 t.	Tor Tørrisson & Lars Amundsson
1857	Røsland	jakt	Severine	65 f. 4 t.	50 f.	19 f.	8 f. 3 t.	Mikkel Larsson Røsland
1857	Innbjoa	jakt	Anne Karine	65 f. 5 t.	50 f.	18 f. 11 t.	8 f. 3 t.	Sjur E. Hetland and Elling Stensen Hetland
1858	Undarheim	jakt	Lina	62 f.	46 f.	18 f. 9 t.	7 f. 9 t.	Johannes Gunnarsson Helland
1863	Kvinnherad	jakt	Maren Kristine?	50 f. 6 t.	39 f.	17 f.	6 f. 5 t.	
1863	Fjelberg	skøite	Lydiana	38 f.	30 f.	16 f.	5 f. 3 t.	
1868	Fjelberg	jakt	Stine Katrine	63 f. 6 t.	50 f. 8 t,	19 f. 6 t.	7 f. 9 t.	Elling Stensen Hetland
1869	Fjelberg	jakt	Familien	51 f. 3 t.	40 f. 3 t.	17 f. 3 t.	7 f.	

Petter Lexau von Tangen

In Bergen in the beginning of the 1800s, Herman von Tangen (1766-1834) continued in the family business of buying fish and selling and exporting fish products. He had several children and five of them became merchants like their father. They all had offices at Tyskebryggen which comprised a long row of merchant offices and warehouses along the harbor in Bergen. The von Tangens had their offices in different buildings as follows.

> Christian Gerhard (1804-1869) – Started his own firm with office in Bredsgården.

> Herman, Jr. (1805-1876) – Started his own firm with office in Holmedalen.

> Johan Lyder (1807-1871) and Christopher (1818-1890) – They took over their father's firm and changed the name to Herman von Tangens Sønner with offices in Dramshusen.

> Petter Lexau (1811-1888) - Started his own firm with office in Solegården.

Petter was a large-scale operator who owned many vessels and shares in others. He is recorded as the occupant of the rooms of stue 3 in Solegården in 1837. He also had warehouses at Sandviken and according to Adolph Berg in Bergen i gamle dage he would make the walk from Tyskebryggen to Sandviken with his friend Hans Didrik Martens to inspect the fish and tran (cod liver oil) works, always arriving there at precisely the same time. Later Petter expanded into the front rooms in stue 1 in Revelsgården, a prime location.

Petter worked with farmer-fishermen to fund their expeditions to the northern fishing grounds and it appears he would step in if a vessel owner needed to be bought out. He was also active in shipping and owned ships and shares of ships. He had the bark *Ludvig Holberg* built in 1867. She was lost in 1873.

Portrait of the bark *Ludvig Holberg*
painted by F. Sørvig in 1868
courtesy of the Bergen Maritime Museum

In December of 1880 Petter von Tangen transferred his firm to Christopher Johannes Hammer von Tangen (1833-) who was the son of Petter's brother, Christian von Tangen. The firm continued as "Petter von Tangen".

Petter died of pneumonia in December of 1888. The group of buildings that included Solegården and Revelsgården was torn down in 1900.

SØSTUERNES FAÇADE

The facade of Solegården and Revelsgården
These buildings extended back about 90 meters and were flanked by similar buildings.
(Søstuernes Façade = Facade of the sea rooms, the rooms facing the water)

Stine Katrine's early travels and an end for the Hetlands

We have attempted to discover the story of Stine Katrine through newspaper accounts, most of which are just a notice that she arrived at, or departed from, a port. This is hardly a substitute for a ship's log and only gives a sketchy picture.

Her first skipper was Johannes Ingebrigtsen and he commanded the following trips, all related to the Nordlands trade.

1869 April 1 - Sailed from Bergen for Finmarken with 200 barrels salt;
1869 May 20 - Sailed past Tromsø from Finmarken;
1870 January 20 - Arrived Bergen from Nordland with 560 barrels herring.
1870 April 11- Sailed past Tromsø on way to Finmarken;
1872 July 10 - Arrived Kristiansund from Ålesund with salt and tran,

In the next period there were several skippers and the notices show trips into the Baltic.

1874 March 11 - Arrived Tromsø from Bergen with salt; skipper Th. Olsen

1875 May 26 - Arrived Pillau, Prussia from Drøbak; Mickelsen

1875 June 14 - Sailed from Pillau to Stavanger; Michelsen

1876 April 5 - Sailed by Tromsø on way to Finmarken from Bergen; Bjerkenæs

1878 May 13 - Left Narva, Estonia for Bergen

1878 June 12 - Arrived Bergen from Narva, Estonia with 580 Tschetwert rye;
   skipper T. Scheveland   (1 Tschetwert = 6 bushels)

In 1880, Petter von Tangen transferred his business to his nephew and the firm continued as 'Petter von Tangen' but the personal relationship between Petter and Elling was probably diminished or lost.

The next skipper is Elling's son, Stine's brother; Elling Ellingsen Hetland. He was born in 1858 and his brother Anton Johan was born in 1861. Both were listed as seamen in the census of 1875 when they were 17 and 14.

The enrollment records for young Elling show that he sailed on *Stine Katrine* from Bergen to Finnmarken and returned over the period from February 18 to April 26, 1881. Then he sailed on *Gjøa* from Bergen to Sweden and returned between June 16 and July 25, 1881. A note indicates that his mandatory naval enrollment was delayed until Sept 30, 1881. He probably got his skipper's certificate at this time which then exempted him from naval service.

Elling Ellingsen Hetland

CJØA af HARDANGER fört af Skipr A. SEXE.

Gjøa in 1875
The owner and skipper was Asbjørn Sexe
Painting by Fredrik Sørvig
Amundsen bought *Gjøa* from Sexe in 1901

The next newspaper notice indicates that Elling was now the skipper of ***Stine Katrine*** at the age of 23.

July 31, 1881- Jagts Lina, Ellingsen; Anne Karine, Larsen; Stine Katrine, Hetland arrived Kristiansund from Bergen with salt and barrels.

[Don't be confused by Ellingsen as skipper of Lina. That is somebody else.]

On the 3rd of February the next year, there was an incident that had serious consequences and our story turns darker. *Stine Katrine* was in the Lofotens for the winter fishery and she and other jakts were caught at anchor in a storm with an onshore wind. On *Stine Katrine* and on the jakt *Vigra*, the crews had to cut away the mast and rigging to keep from being blown ashore. Another jakt lost her bowsprit. This jakt and *Stine Katrine* were referred to as belonging to Petter von Tangen. This incident would mean the loss of an important season and serious financial loss. The next we know is that, in 1882, exactly a year after the near shipwreck, Elling Ellingsen died in Haugesund. The cause was reported as pneumonia.

In 1883 Elling Stensen was in financial trouble. There was a claim against him in July. In March of 1884, the skøite[8] *Forsøget* had to be sold at auction as part of the settlement.

Tvangsauktion.

Tirsdagen den 25. Marts førstk. Eftermiddag Kl. 5, bliver efter Forlangende af Sagfører Bonnevie Angell, paa Vedkommendes Vegne, paa Rekvirentens Kontor i 20 Rode No. 40 a, afholdt offentlig Tvangsauktion over den her paa Havnen henliggende Skøite „Forsøget", der ved Exekutionsforretning den 10de Juli f. A. er udlagt hos Elling Stensen Hetland og A. Fjelberg.

Enhver Vedkommende advares om under Auktionen at varetage sit Tarv.

Bergens Auktionsdirektørs Kontor, den 25. Februar 1884.

C. Nergaard, kst.

---

[8] A skøite is smaller than a jakt and has a similar rig. But the skøite has a sharp stern instead of a transom stern. Most had a platform built on the stern to provide deck space like a jakt.

At some point the firm 'Petter von Tangen' took over *Stine Katrine*. Then Elling Stensen died on April 29, 1884 of pneumonia. Could an illness have contributed to financial failure or did the financial failure lead to death? Later that year, in July, a bankruptcy auction was held where his belongings were to be sold and were listed as:

"...consisting of cattle and sheep, bedclothes and walking clothes, furnishings of iron and wood, gold, silver, brass and copper, equipment of boat and net, inventory, along with the estate's two sea houses [warehouses on the wharf] on leased land at Innbjoa where a general store was operated for a number of years."

His son by his second wife, Edvard Ellingsen Hetland, purchased the farm and the family has been successful there ever since.

Stine's story

The namesake of our subject vessel also had an interesting but tough life. Stine was the first child in the family then came three brothers: Sten, Elling and Anton. In 1862, when Stine was 9, their mother died. The same year their father married Berta Ragnhilde Endresdatter Eide from Sand. They had three more children: Edvard, Karl Johan, and Berta. In 1867 their mother, Berta Ragnhilde, died. She was only 25 and Stine was just 13. The next year was big for Stine, she had a jakt named for her and she was confirmed in the church.

At the age of 18 she married Endre Olsen Eide from Sand, a relation of Berta Ragnhilde, and they lived in Sand where Endre eventually took over his mother's farm. Sand was in Ryfylke on the Boknafjord which had no navigable connection to the Hardangerfjord.

Stine, Endre and the two oldest children, Bertha (Bertine) and Anna Karine, moved to Bjoa sometime between 1875-1877, most likely to live on Elling Stensen Hetland's farm. Endre ran Elling's barrel factory but that went bankrupt for a lack of demand since the herring fishery had declined. 1875 had been a great year for the northern herring fishery but in 1876 the herring disappeared. Stine and Endre decided to return to Sand and the farm that Endre owned. Stine was pregnant again and the family's economy was not good. For reasons we do not know for sure, possibly because of their financial situation, they decide that Bertha, who is 4 or 5 years old, will be left with grandfather Elling and aunts and uncles at Hetland. But Bertha didn't want this, she understood that her parents and sister would be leaving without her. Stine and Endre decided instead to leave little Anne Karine who doesn't understand what is happening.

America fever was gripping Norway. Endre had a brother and a sister who emigrated to Illinois and Iowa in 1880. Stine had aunts and uncles on both her father's side and her mother's side who were well established in Iowa and Illinois. Stine and Endre decided to go to America and Endre sold the farm. In

June of 1880 he was recorded as being a "jægtefører", a jakt captain, while on previous occasions he was listed as a farmer. (In Ryfylke a jakt was called a jekt or jægt, not to be confused with the Nordlands jekt.)

Two jakts in Sandvikja at Sand

In June of 1881, they said goodbye to family and friends at Sand, and went to Hetland to pick up Anna Karine to take her to America. She had not seen her parents since she was two years old and hardly remembered them. The family she knows is grandfather Elling and Stine's brothers and sister. Anna Karine did not want to go to America, no matter how much the parents tried. Amazingly, they let that 5-year-old girl choose her path through life and she stayed in Norway.

Anna Karine grew up with her grandfather Elling, and after he died, with her uncle, Edvard, who didn't marry until some years later. She remembered all her life that she did not want to go to America. Her grandchildren often asked if she missed her mother and her father and she always answered no. She had a good upbringing with her family at Hetland. Even though she did not miss Stine and Endre, she missed having a mother. Anna Karine married and there are now more descendants of hers in Norway than from all of Stine's other children together.

Stine and Endre took a steamship to America, a trip that would take about two weeks. They had their hands full since Elen was only one year old, Ole was 2 ½, and Bertha was 8. They first lived in Ellsworth, Iowa among many Norwegians. After 1885 they moved to Astoria, Oregon where Endre worked as a longshoreman. Endre changed his name to Andrew and the family name to Eade. They had five more children for a total of eight living in the U.S. They were in Astoria in 1900 but later moved back to Ellsworth. Stine died there in 1907 at the age of 53. Andrew lived on to be 89.

Anna Karine, their daughter in Norway

Andrew and his daughters in America.

A new home in Jondal

Jondal on the Hardangerfjord was a small community but it came to have a large fleet of jakts and other similar vessels. Around 1900 almost every household in Jondal had a skipper, or sailor, or vessel owner living there. Harbors farther along the fjord, all the way to Odda, were also home to jakts but the fjord could freeze and there were times when those vessels were hindered and even damaged by the ice. Jondal was free from ice.

Stine Katrine was bought by a group in Jondal in 1891 and that was her home port for more than forty years. She continued in the Nordlands trade as well the herring fishery at Espever, Røver og Batalden. Ole Underhaug was the skipper and manager until, in 1896, she was sold by Underhaug and his partners to another group in Jondal. The purchase contract lists the owners and their shares in the vessel which is shown in tables below. Two of the men appear in both groups. Their occupations and ages come from census records. The purchase price was 4193 kroner.

Sellers in 1896	Occupation and relationship	Age
Ole Olsen Underhaug	managing owner and skipper	42
Kristoffer Oddsen Underhaug	farmer, stone cutter	41
Ivar P. Brække	stone cutter	47
Torsten S. Vik	farmer	44
Olai L. Sætvedt	pilot of steamships	30
Ole Larsen Torsnæs	farmer	-

Buyers in 1896	Occupation and relationship	Age	Shares
Kristian Thorbjørnsen Prestegaard	managing owner and skipper	28	9/48
Tobias Thorbjørnsen Prestegaard	brother of Kristian; owner and skipper of slupp *Heimdal*	25	9/48
Edvard Fjærtoft	lensmann (sheriff); partner in other vessels	41	6/48
Johan Bakke	merchant	29	6/48
Torbjørn Selsvik	Skipper, father-in-law of Tobias	50	6/48
Odd Thorbjørnsen Prestegaard	brother of Kristian	36	4/48
Olai Sætvedt	pilot of steamships	30	4/48
Torsten Vik	farmer	44	4/48

1894 had been a year of large financial losses due to too many fish buyers on the grounds and low prices when they came to sell their cargo to the exporters. Many boats from the large fleet from Tysnes were sold off but the folks at Jondal held out. The following year was a record year for fishing in the Lofotens with the catch declining in the years thereafter.

In October of 1904, *Stine Katrine* was entered in the Bergen Ship Registry. At the time she lay in the harbor at Kristiansund. The change in registry required a lot of paperwork and fortunately the papers are preserved in the state archives in Stavanger.

We found that the skipper, Kristian Prestegaard died of tuberculosis (lungetæring) in Hammerfest in June of 1905. He must have continued to sail even when sick but then had to go ashore to a hospital in Hammerfest, far from home. His death at 37 prompted the other owners to sell *Stine Katrine* except that Tobias kept his share. All of the new owners were from Jondal except Ole Johnsen who was from Tysnes. They paid 3333 kroner for 5/6 shares with Tobias holding 1/6 shares so, the total value was 4000 kroner.

Buyers in 1906	Occupation and relationship	Age	Shares
Jakob Salomonsen Belsnæs	managing owner	42	1/6
Ole Johnsen Øvrevaage	skipper	62	1/6
Daniel Salomonsen Belsnæs	skipper of jakt *Mathilde*, then captain of steamship *Ernst* brother of Jakob	38	1/6
Ivar S. Borgen		38	1/6
Sjur S. Borgen		36	1/6
Tobias T. Prestegaard	continuing as part owner	35	1/6

In 1912 Ole Johnsen sold his share in **Stine Katrine** to Samson Gundtvedt for 550 kroner. Samson became the skipper until she was sold in 1935. Previously he was skipper in the jakt **Marthilde** (not **Mathilde**) from 1901 to 1911. **Marthilde** had been built in 1875 and was sold away from Jondal in 1912.

A view of the harbor at Jondal in 1907.
The jakt on the right has been identified as Marthilde.
The jakt on her left could be Stine Katrine.
Photo by Knud Knudsen, courtesy of the University in Bergen.

34

A water level view of the same scene.
Marthilde can be read on the nameboard of the jakt closest.
The name of the other jakt is not legible. It could be ***Stine Katrine***.
Photo by Knud Knudsen, courtesy of the University in Bergen.

In 1918 *Stine Katrine* was rebuilt in Hatlestrand on the other side of the fjord not far from Jondal.

In 1924 Odd Prestegaard sold his share to Torolf Guntvedt for 500 kroner.

In 1926 Kristoffer Sollesnes bought a 1/12 share from the widow of Daniel Belsnæs who had died in 1913.

As steamship services improved and the crews could take a steamship to and from the fishing grounds, the jakts no longer had to return to their home port and often remained in Kristiansund. Also, in the 1920s and 30s the northern fisheries changed significantly. Instead of selling to buy-boats like *Stine Katrine*, fishermen delivered their fish directly to processors on land and the processed fish went to market in steamships. Sailing jakts became less and less useful and the harbor at Kristiansund was crowded with laid-up jakts. Many were scrapped or burned. A few were bought and converted to motor power. *Stine Katrine* was one of the lucky ones and was bought by a freight operator. Having been rebuilt in 1918, she was probably in relatively good condition compared to other jakts.

In September of 1935, the partners in Jondal sold *Stine Katrine* to Andreas Fenstad of Stadsbygd for 4000 kroner. It is remarkable how the boat's value remained constant since 1891. *Stine Katrine* was the last sailing jakt that called Jondal home.

Looking aft on the deck of a jakt in Lofoten. The crew are dressing cod.
The young man on the left in uniform must be the owner's son.
From an old postcard.

Åsta 1

Andreas Fenstad, the son of Johan Iversen, was a skipper who operated a small fleet of freight boats which sailed mostly between Trøndelag and northern Norway. The fleet was based in Stadsbygd which lies east of Trondheim across the fjord. One of his freight boats was *Pilot*, a ketch rigged cutter.

Andreas bought *Stine Katrine* from the partners in Jondal for 4000 kroner in September of 1935. She was laying at Kristiansund at the time. He named her *Åsta 1*; Åsta being the name of his ten-year-old daughter as well as his younger sister. The number "1" appears because there was already a vessel named Åsta. Fenstad installed an engine and turned her into a motor vessel. The first engine was a used one-cylinder June-Munktell semi-diesel with 40 horsepower. See the Appendix for engine data.

The one picture we found shows that she still has her original mast and bowsprit and that a foresail could probably be set, but the rest of her rig is gone. From the measurements on the tonnage certificate, it does not appear that she had a pilothouse at first, but one was added later as seen in the picture.

In 1944, at Kristiansund, *Åsta 1* was struck by a German patrol boat and sank. She was later raised and repaired and continued to haul freight, including cargos of tørrfisk and klippfisk from Lofoten. This is probably when a 70 horsepower Deutz diesel was installed.

In July of 1948 Fenstad sold *Åsta 1* to the firm A/S Ramsvik & Eidsaune in Råkvåg, Stjørna for 40,000 kroner. Ramsvik & Eidsaune were fish merchants who specialized in herring. They owned a saltery, their own boats and fishing gear. One of their boats was the 48-foot fishing cutter *Rolf 1*. At this time a much larger engine was installed in *Åsta 1*. It was a used, Swedish-made June Munktell with 120 horsepower.

Åsta 1 under motor power
Photo from Bjugn Bygnatun

In the care of the Hidle family

At the entrance to the Hardangerfjord is the island of Bømlo and on a narrow part of the island is a parcel of land that has been recorded as Hidle since 1518. As folk adopted hereditary surnames, many people there adopted Hidle for their surname. Nils Sigurd Hidle was born at Hidle in 1890 and went by the name Sigurd. His family owned a large tract of land in Hidle and after his father died, he bought the farm from the other heirs. Sigurd had eight children with his wife Anna. The youngest was Tolleiv (Tolleif) was born in 1938 and he recorded the family history in his book Treet vårt (Our tree) published in 2016.

In 1936 Sigurd Hidle bought the motor cutter *Goxheim* which became an important part of the family economy. *Goxheim* was used for herring fishing and for carrying freight as well as towing barges of limestone from Moster on Bømlo to Odda at the very end of the Hardangerfjord. Hidle was in a good location near the entrance to the Kulleseid Canal which provided access to the sea side of the island. Sigurd's son Arthur took over *Goxheim* in 1960 and operated a shuttle service from Bjoa to the shipyard on Stord where he worked.

The Hidle Family

Third row: sons Lars, Arthur, Hans, Sverre
Second row: daughters Nelly, Sissi, Konstanse
First row: mother Anna, son Tollief, father Nils Sigurd

In August of 1951, three of the brothers, Hans, Arthur, and Lars, and their father, Nils Sigurd, came together and bought *Åsta 1* for 90,000 kroner. They planned to use her to transport herring from the fishing grounds and registered her with the Fisheries Directorate. She was assigned the mark H-61-M (Hordaland-61-Moster). Next, they wanted a new name for her; *Åsta 1* didn't suit their corner of the world. Hans was the manager for the boat and was married to Anna Kjerstine. After some discussion the group came up with *Anne Kristine* which seemed to fit an aging Hardanger jakt[9]. The name change took effect in July of 1952.

Tolleif was 13 when *Anne Kristine* arrived and he thought their new boat was a strange sight with a tall mast and a little pilothouse. *Anne Kristine* was modified to have a large pilothouse set on a deckhouse, a shorter mast and a bigger cargo hatch. At 15 Tolleif came onboard as cook and, over three and a half years, he developed into a "cooking-proficient engineer, well familiar with the coast".

I asked Tolleif what *Anne Kristine* was used for. Below is my interpretation of his answer:

> You ask what loads *Anne Kristine* transported. It was everything. It's almost easier to write what she did not carry. When she came into our family, Norway was being rebuilt after the war and there was plenty of freight to be carried. There was cement in bags and fertilizer from eastern Norway going westbound and scrap iron and tin waste from canneries going eastbound. Then there was building material and lumber westbound. *Anne Kristine* transported a lot of fiber cement panels; both corrugated and flat. I remember well that the first load I went along with was flour in 50 kg. sacks going from Stavanger to

---

[9] Similarly, in 1977, Hans van de Vooren took on the task of restoring the jakt Dyrafjeld and he too came up with a new name which suited an old jakt; Anna Kristina. By this time Anne Kristine was in Swedish ownership.]

Grimstad. An episode I also remember was a load of crates. One crate we dropped down in the hold and the crate broke open and out came weapons marked with swastikas. We nailed the box together and delivered it to Oslo. January, February, and March it was herring transport, mostly from Måløy and Florø to Haugesund. The rest of the year it was in and out of all the fjords from the Swedish coast and up to Trøndelag. I was onboard when we saved a boat that had broken down off the Stad peninsula. We got a towline on the boat before it went into the rocky cliffs and towed it to Ålesund. I started onboard as a 15-year-old and, on my 18th birthday, I was alone on duty and followed the beacons through the narrow straits in the middle of the black night.

Some years later, in 1963, Tolleif set out to build a house in Husa, south of Hidle. He cut the timber from his own woodland at Husa and used Anne Kristine to tow the logs to a sawmill in Ølen. He then brought back the finished lumber as well as cement and sand to the building site.

In 1963 the June-Munktell engine, which dated from 1938, was replaced with a used Wichmann 2AB engine which had the same power but was newer by nine years. The Wichmann factory was nearby at Rubbestadneset on Bømlo and their engines were common in the local boats. See the Appendix for the story on the engine. In 1971 Tolleif took a job at Wichmann and worked there until retirement.

The Sauholmen brothers

Hans Hidle sold Anne Kristine to Jan-Henry Sauholmen in July of 1968 for 30,000 kroner. Jan Henry worked with his brother Einar and were based at Eikelandsosen. Jan-Henry wrote that they and "carried a lot of odd things, also sand and stone." They had problems with leakage like the other owners.

Anne Kristine at Eikelandsosen

Sauholmen sold her to Göran Grauers of Sweden in August 1973 for 40,000 kroner. Permission had to be obtained to sell *Anne Kristine* out of Norway. Riksantikvaren and the Bergen Maritime Museum were consulted to determine if the vessel was important for the preservation of Norwegian culture. The sale was approved but might have not been a few years earlier. Amundsen's jakt,

Gjøa, had lain at San Francisco for many years leaving a gap in the collection at the Norwegian National Maritime Museum. A jakt like *Anne Kristine* was considered for display to fill the gap. Fortunately, *Gjøa* was returned to Norway in 1972 on the deck of a cargo ship. In 1974 Jan Henry bought a steel vessel and named it *Sauholm* and continued their freight business. The vessel's previous name was *Sagholm* so the name change was rather easy. Jan Henry went on to be a captain in HSD, the company which provided ferry service in the Hardanger area. Einar continued the family boat building and repair business.

«Anne-Kristine», bygget som jakt i 1869, og ganske lik «Gjøa», i meget god stand, selges da jeg vil ha større båt. Adresse: Jan-Henry Sauholmen, 5672 Bergegrend.

Classified ad from Aftenposten, June 9, 1972
Jan-Henry offers Anne Kristine for sale.
Translation: "**Anne Kristine**" built as a jakt in 1869, and rather like "Gjøa", in very good condition, to be sold since I want a bigger boat.

Anne Kristine looking good after a recent paint job.

She returns to sail under the Swedish flag

The following is a summary of events in the life of *Anne Kristine* when she was owned by Göran Grauers. It is a digest of a manuscript written by Grauers (150+ pages in Swedish) with some additions from correspondence. The goal of this summary is to capture the movements of *Anne Kristine* and the steps taken to convert her back to a sailing vessel. The manuscript was not complete and did not cover the sale of *Anne Kristine*. Very few dates were provided. Dates have been added where they could reasonably be determined. Some information has been added such as the name of the hurricane Fran. Place names have been changed to agree with current spellings. The reader is encouraged to follow the many legs of the journey with a searchable map service like Google maps.

Göran Grauers grew up in Stocksund, Sweden in a middle-class, well-off home. He hadn't found much direction in life. He tried the military but that didn't work out. In 1972 he had been employed as a bus driver for almost two years. He had sailed dinghies and larger family sailboats and had sailed the canals of Holland and France as crew. In 1972 he was in Spain and was moving his father's 37-foot sloop from Motril to Jávea. On that trip he met Keith Floyd who was a celebrity chef in the UK. Floyd told Grauers about buying an old fishing boat in Norway and how they were plentiful and cheap. Grauers also had fond memories of sailing on a galeas (a larger, ketch-rigged version of a jakt) in Stocksund. He began to think about finding a boat for himself in Norway and using her for a world cruise. He had an inheritance that could cover the cost of a boat but he had to get his father to release the money.

He spent weeks in Norway looking for the right boat with the help of a broker. He finally found his perfect boat in *Anne Kristine* but had to wait for a previous buyer to drop out. At this point *Anne Kristine* was still a motor-powered cargo boat with no sailing rig. At the end of July in 1973 the deal was made and he took delivery in August. He wanted to start his world cruise right away after an outfit period in Portugal and gathered a crew of four with that in mind. He thought Portugal would offer low prices and a good climate. Also, he knew there were many laid-up vessels and perhaps he could purchase a rig from one of them.

Grauers and his crew took delivery of *Anne Kristine* at Hjellestad, a few miles south of Bergen. They stayed at Hjellestad a week while they removed the cargo winch to sell back. They loaded sand in the hold as ballast. Trucks dumped four loads totaling 32 metric tons directly in the hold.

They met an old man who had sailed on *Stine Katrine* when he was young. He said that with a crew of only three they sailed as far as Gibraltar. The old sailor bragged about her speed claiming they had sailed at an average speed of 13 knots for three days.

With preparations complete, Grauers and his crew set out but they were met with bad weather rounding the southern end of Norway and put in at Flekkefjord. When the weather improved, they motored on to Uddevalla, Sweden. In Sweden, Grauers found that customs would require him to pay VAT (Value Added Tax) and duty on the vessel. They gave him fourteen days to leave without having to pay so he loaded up with materials for the rebuilding and left for Portugal. He had already planned out the work during the summer. On deck were secured five drums of diesel fuel and a drum of oil.

They motored south through the Kattegat to Kiel, Germany. On the approach to Kiel, they were almost run down by a trawler. In Kiel they loaded on a new Lister generator, rated at 7.5 kW, along with a big load of beer and spirits. In Brunsbüttel, at the west end of the Kiel Canal, they met Bror Pettersson and his crew on the fishing boat Elaiza from Gotland, Sweden. They were about to try a fishing charter in the Canary Islands. Pettersson and Grauers agreed to keep in company on the voyage to Portugal.

They left Brunsbüttel with Elaiza but the sea was high and *Anne Kristine* was not making progress so they entered Cuxhaven. The harbor was inhospitable so they went to sea again and reached Cherbourg. They lay there for three weeks waiting for better weather. When it came, they began a calm crossing of the Bay of Biscay. However, they didn't reach Spain before the weather deteriorated again, this time due to Hurricane Fran which had tracked straight across the Atlantic aiming for Brittany. This was in October 1973. After a frightening overnight struggle through high seas, they reached the little fishing port of Cariño, at the northwest corner of Spain.

After leaving Cariño they were going to enter Porto, Portugal but Grauers got a bad feeling and turned away then proceeded to Lisbon. Grauers had major problems with port authorities in Lisbon over the ship's papers since she had not yet been registered in Sweden. One result was that they had to fly the Norwegian flag while they were there. Three of the four crew had had enough and left. A fellow named Perre stayed on. Conditions were not favorable at Lisbon and they moved across the river to Seixal. They removed the sand ballast and succeeded in finding a steel mast from a sunken German sailboat. The mast was secured to the deck of *Anne Kristine* to be installed later.

At Christmas time he decided to move on to southern Spain. Marianne, his girlfriend, and Hector, his brother, had joined him and Perre. The oil embargo had hit Portugal in late November and fuel was impossible to obtain. They left with 2 hours of fuel hoping to reach Cadiz. It turned out to be barely enough. Here they refueled and headed for Gibraltar and reached it in time to celebrate the new year.

In Gibraltar they decided to go to Motril to start work. They took on a big load of beer and spirits again. When they got to Motril they found they weren't welcome since they had come from British Gibraltar. They left for Almeria in the hope of finding a suitable shipyard but without success. The went on to Santa Pola where they found a shipyard that could haul and repair the hull.

They decided on Torreveija to do the topside and interior work. Here there was plenty of space for them to work. Hector and Perre left. With help of new friends, Eje and Pär, the masts were raised and the interior was finished. *Anne Kristine* was being transformed into a staysail schooner, a yacht rig and hardly a traditional rig for a jakt. It appears that the mainmast and boom were steel and the other spars were wood. The foremast was kept and a topmast added to it. They spent a year and a half at Torreveija.

Grauers took her to Denia to be hauled, scraped, re-caulked, and painted. Grauers took this opportunity to go back to Sweden but while he was gone progress stopped over a political issue. Five terrorists had been executed by Franco's regime in Spain in September 1975. The Swedish prime minister, Olaf Palme, condemned this action and the regime so anything Swedish was not welcome in Spain. *Anne Kristine* sat on the ways for 45 days without being worked on while she dried out and opened up. Finally, the political situation calmed down, the hull work was finished and *Anne Kristine* was launched. The next big job was to remove the deckhouse. There still remained work to make booms and gaffs and set up the running rigging. Marianne had left and Grauers met Lili, an English woman, who, it turned out, was wanted for robbery.

After Franco died in November 1975 the situation changed again and Grauers was given a deadline to leave. Several items had been stolen from Grauers' storeroom and the shipyard was installed replacements and tried to charge him for them, a bill he couldn't pay. They left Denia quietly very early in the morning mixed in with the local fishboats and headed for Sardinia. A sirocco blew up and the next two days were a struggle. It was all Grauers could do to keep the boat pumped out. They reached Carloforte on the Italian island of San Pietro. There they tried to do charter sailing without luck. Eventually the authorities showed up with a large bill for port charges. In the fall of 1976, he and Lili decided to travel back to Sweden to earn some money. They got married. He drove a taxi.

He and Lili returned to Carloforte seven months later with a crew of 10 with the intention of sailing back to Sweden. After some difficulties with the port authorities, they departed. They reached Mallorca and were hauled out and a major leak was fixed. The running rigging was put in order while waiting to go to the shipyard. After leaving Mallorca they managed to set all the sails for the first time. They were sailing well on a course to Jávea in the night when a blast of wind hit the boat wrecking the rig and breaking the rudder at the waterline. As they tried to get the torn sails down another blast hit and a crewman suffered severe rope burns. They entered Jávea where the crew left. The plans for a voyage to Sweden were ruined. Two Englishmen became the next crew. With their help, the boat was ready to sail in two weeks and they headed for Gibraltar in hopes of getting charter work.

Finally, under full sail

Photo courtesy of Göran Grauers

At an unknown port; Photo courtesy of Göran Grauers

She had a large, homey salon; Photo courtesy of Göran Grauers

They laid at Gibraltar for three months. It turned out that there was no charter market and the Lister generator was out of commission. Grauers and Lili went to England for three months then Grauers went on to Sweden where drove a taxi for three months. Here he decided that the goal was the West Indies and not just to get back to Sweden. They returned to Gibraltar then sailed on to Vilamoura, Portugal. There they got some charter work even though it was not legal for a foreign vessel. They were encouraged to go to Madeira. However, the laws against them doing charters were strengthened and they only managed a few charters, enough to buy food. They had an encounter with the police where Grauers was threatened with jail. They determined to move on to Gran Canaria. They landed at Las Palmas but there was no room at the quay so they sailed on to Puerto Rico on the south side of the island. Here, John Berke, a freelance photographer, appeared wanting to do a story on *Anne Kristine*. The article appeared in the Norwegian magazine "Alle Menn". Apparently Grauers never saw the article. The photograph in the article shows him with a big smile and a large, bushy, blond head of hair.

A Swedish man, Kennet, showed up and was willing to invest some money to ensure his passage to Trinidad for Carnival. They arranged for time in the shipyard at Lanzarote in December. But now there was trouble with the main engine. A crankshaft bearing had wiped from lack of oil. New bearings were cast in babbit by a company in Las Palmas and after some heavy work the engine was running again. They took a three-week dive charter then *Anne Kristine* was hauled at the yard on Lanzarote with satisfactory results. And now a puppy was added to the crew.

Back in Puerto Rico they began preparations for a transatlantic crossing. *Anne Kristine* now had a crew of 12 men, most of which were so-called "back packers". In addition, two young English girls with no sailing experience, Debbi and Sharon, showed up and asked to join. They departed for the Cape Verde Islands but were caught in a storm. They backtracked and found refuge in the harbor at Santa Cruz on Tenerife. They waited three weeks in Santa Cruz hoping for better weather. Several of the crew left and they were down to nine.

The voyage to St. Vincent was calm and windless. Kennet left under bad terms taking the charts and navigational instruments with him. More crew left so it was down to Grauers, Lili, Sharon and Debbi. They finally departed St. Vincent with a reef in the main and under power. They had 2000 miles to go and had fuel for 1400. On the 17th day they arrived in Bridgetown, Barbados. The Danish school ship *Danmark* was in the harbor and *Anne Kristine* made a good impression when she sailed in and anchored nearby.

Grauers doesn't mention it but they also shared the anchorage with *Sofia*, a three-masted Baltic schooner. *Sofia* was a true hippie vessel and Pamela Bitterman writes about her experiences on board in her book Sailing for the Horizon. In it she describes *Anne Kristine* and her crew. Grauers used the name George while in the Caribbean. They spent nine months in Barbados and the condition of *Anne Kristine* was poor. They scheduled time in the drydock at Fort de France, Martinique and stopped at St. Lucia on the way.

They moved on to St. Thomas where they were allowed to charter. They found a niche in serving the crews of the cruise ships, sometimes five ships in a week. In 1980 Grauers got a contract to do major repairs on a wooden catamaran and came away with a decent profit. *Anne Kristine* continued to deteriorate and to hide the rust stains she was painted black.

In the last paragraph of the manuscript Grauers wrote that he was going to the West End of Tortola to check out a new shipyard and to see if *Anne Kristine* could be hauled there. He got a job in that shipyard and hauled her there but she didn't leave her mooring for a year and a half.

In 1982 Grauers offered *Anne Kristine* for sale and placed an ad in Woodenboat Magazine. While he claimed she was a sistership to Gjøa that was not true. She was similar but they were built at different times by different builders. After nine years of struggles with a leaky ship he finally parted with her, but the sale went badly and he ended up with nothing.

A once-in-a-lifetime opportunity. The 113-year-old NORWEGIAN JAKT, Anne-Kristine, sistership to Raoul Amundsen's GJOA. 73' x 20' x 10'6". Rebuilt 1974-76. Trunnel fastened Norwegian pine on oak. 5 private staterooms, huge salon, new sails and rig 1975. Contact George Grauers, c/o White, P.O. Box 641, Roadtown, Tortola, BVI.

Anne Kristine comes to the U.S.

Just like her original namesake, the little girl Stine Katrine, *Anne Kristine* eventually came to the United States. She was resurrected through the tremendous efforts of Norman Baker and his family and reached the United States which would be her home for years.

Baker was a civil engineer but more importantly an adventurer, a flyer and a deep-water sailor. He had naval experience from serving on destroyers during the Korean conflict. In 1955, he was the navigator on an expedition in Tahiti when he met and befriended Thor Heyerdahl. When Heyerdahl planned his reed boat expedition with RA for 1969, he brought Baker on board as navigator and second in command. Baker stayed on for the RA II expedition in 1970 and for the Tigris expedition in 1978. He would be an explorer and adventurer for the rest of his life.

Norman Baker and Thor Heyerdahl

Since that time Baker had been looking for a special boat with which to circumnavigate the world with his family. He wanted an "historic, classic ship". Baker saw the ad for *Anne Kristine* in Woodenboat. The thought of obtaining a vessel like the explorer Amundsen's *Gjøa* must have been a strong attraction. He and his wife, Mary Ann, flew to Tortola to inspect her. The boat was large and roomy and well suited for their complement of five but was in rather poor shape. One of the most striking things from the pictures at that time was that the ship's wheel was broken and pieced together with scraps of lumber. Baker hired a professional surveyor to inspect her. It is not clear what the surveyor reported as to the condition of the hull. It must not have been too discouraging since Baker planned for two months of work to get it in shape. The purchase was complete in 1983. He had arranged to support Thor Heyerdahl on an expedition to the Maldives using *Anne Kristine* as a base ship. But the condition of the vessel was so much worse than anticipated that the schedule and plans to meet Heyerdahl fell apart.

Anne Kristine was hauled out on a railway on Frenchman's Cay (at Soper's Hole) and Norman and his son Daniel (age 22) started work using local shipwrights. The rest of the family, Mary Ann, Elizabeth (age 20) and Mitchell (age 19), flew to Tortola to join them in August; all planning for a two-year circumnavigation. Supplies for the voyage were also on the way. But *Anne Kristine* was in much worse condition than Norman had ever imagined. Much of the topside planking was replaced and 45 frames had to be sistered. The breasthook and transom knees were replaced with natural crooks found on the island. The sampson posts, a deck beam and a beam across the transom had to be replaced. The interior had to be gutted. New water tanks were designed by Norman and fabricated in the U.S. Tons of concrete ballast was added to the bilge in small batches. Mary Ann worked as hard as anyone else and did thankless tasks like cleaning the bilges. She also corresponded with former owners in Norway.

When their attention turned to the rig, Daniel found that the foremast and bowsprit were rotten. When the stays were undone, the foremast broke and fell over from its own weight. The bowsprit, a one-piece spar, was cut off. Further inspection revealed that all the spars had to be replaced. Norman planned to create a workboat schooner rig, different from Grauer's design which was a staysail schooner suited for a yacht. There would be gaff-rigged sails on the fore and main masts and a topmast on each mast. She would have a proper bowsprit with a jibboom (copied from Gjøa). Finding timber for spars was a huge challenge but Norman learned of a stock of powerline poles that was available in Florida. They were of Douglas fir from Oregon and each pole was 80 feet long so they were difficult to ship. Also, a crane was needed and the nearest was on St. Thomas. The solution was to get the poles to St. Thomas on the deck of a cargo ship and have the work done there. The job to shape the spars was given to a local spar builder but within days he and his helper were sickened by the preservative in the poles and quit. Norman and family took on the job and moved *Anne Kristine* to St. Thomas. This was the first time that they started and used the engine. They camped on the unfinished boat without a stove or sink. With the help of two workers from Tortola they did the work of shaping the spars while protecting themselves from the preservative.

Three months after coming to St. Thomas and a year after they realized they had to replace them, the spars were stepped and much of the standing rigging was in place. They motored back to Tortola with the masts held by only one shroud on each side. *Anne Kristine* began to roll and snapped the shrouds on the main mast. Only an iron mast partner kept the mast from tearing out of the boat. The cabin top was badly damaged. After they got back to Tortola the Baker siblings returned to the United States.

In November of 1984 Hurricane Klaus struck Tortola with 75 mile per hour winds. Norman and Mary Ann set three anchors and fought to keep their vessel intact through the night. In the morning a calm set in but it turned out to be the eye of the storm. The wind rose again and struck from the other direction. Many boats were cast ashore during the storm but *Anne Kristine* fared well. The Bakers were exhausted and Norman's hands were injured from struggles with the rigging.

The next big job was to finish the bulwarks and cap rails. This was done by shipwrights Jim and Dolph Smith but at this point the Baker's money had run out. Jim and Dolph graciously finished the job without pay. In 1985 the Bakers sold their home in New Rochelle and committed to life aboard *Anne Kristine*. Volunteers from the local yachting community now came to help with rigging spars and bending on sails, newly made to suit her new rig. The iron work was modeled after plans of Gjøa.

With the vessel nearly complete, the Baker siblings came back in anticipation of their world voyage. In 1986 the family started out under power but after only 16 miles a main bearing in the engine burned out. The bearing had to be custom made and it would be four months before *Anne Kristine* was underway again. Their time and funds were exhausted and the circumnavigation was now out of the question. The Bakers received an invitation to be in the Operation Sail parade to celebrate the centennial of the Statue of Liberty. They decided to accept as a sort of consolation and set sail for New York in June. They arrived fifteen days later on July first and proudly sailed in the parade of ships on the fourth

At this point the Bakers had no direction. At Daniel's request they sailed for Nantucket where Daniel had a job lined up. Meanwhile, as the Bakers pondered their future, South Street Seaport invited them to be an exhibit ship. The invitation was accepted and this provided free dockage through next June. New York became *Anne Kristine*'s new home port. In the spring the Bakers found gainful employment for *Anne Kristine* as a sail training ship out of Halifax for the Sea Venture Society.

In spite of all their difficulties, Norman and Mary Ann loved *Anne Kristine* and would always call her by name not just "the boat".

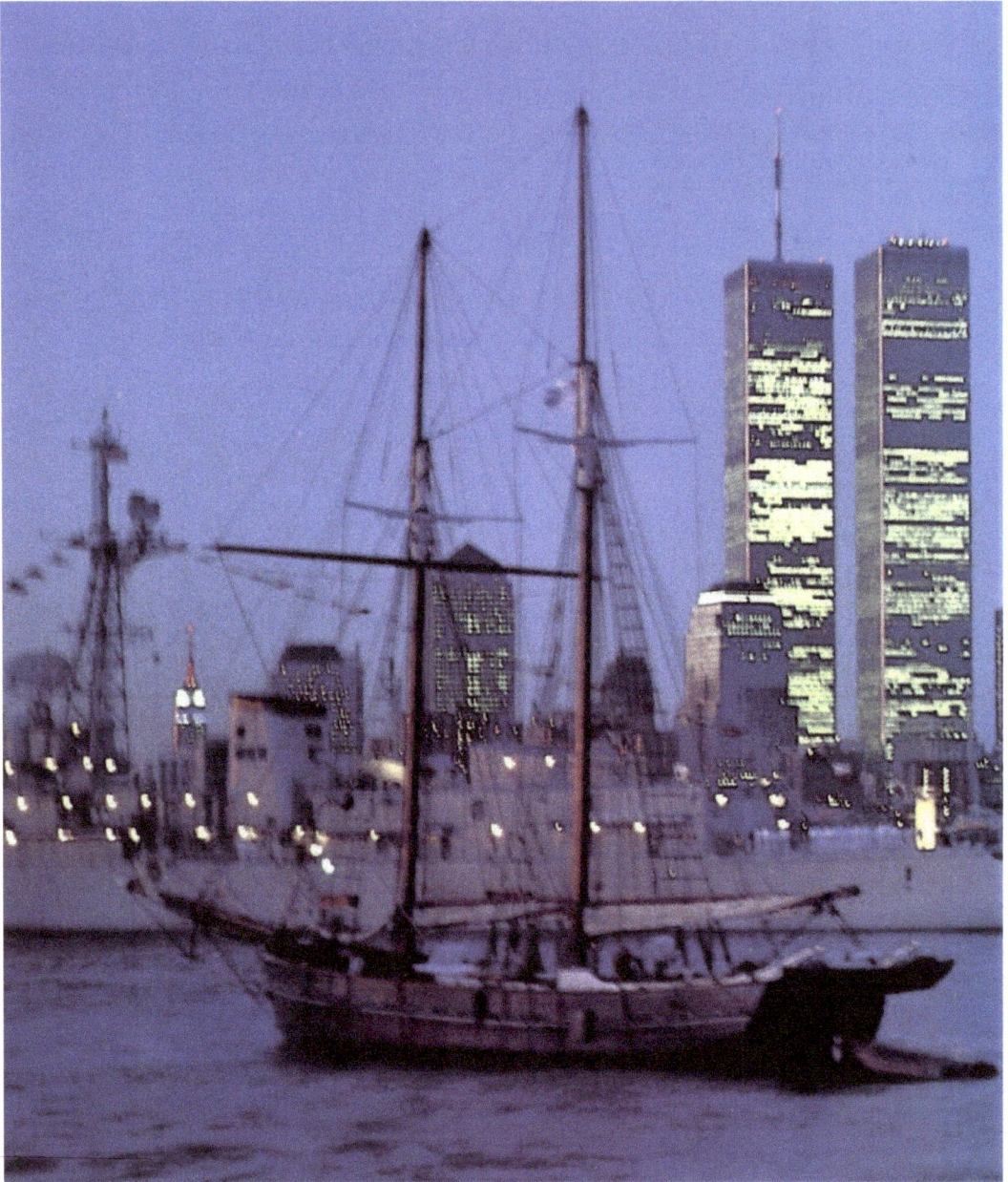

Anne Kristine in New York Harbor for Operation Sail 1986

Anne Kristine in Canadian waters
showing the flag of Canada on her shrouds as a courtesy.

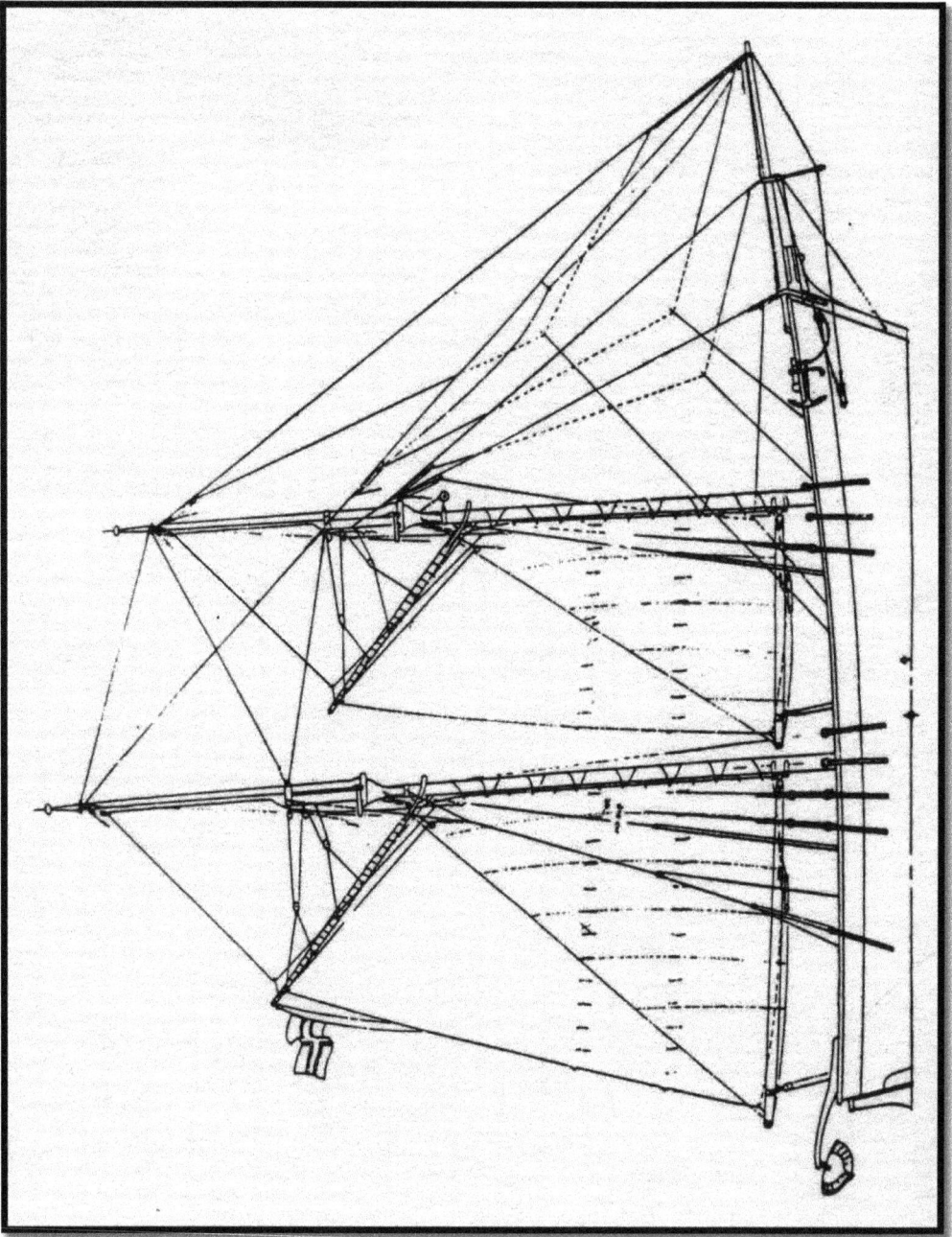

Profile drawing from the Baker's marketing brochure

66

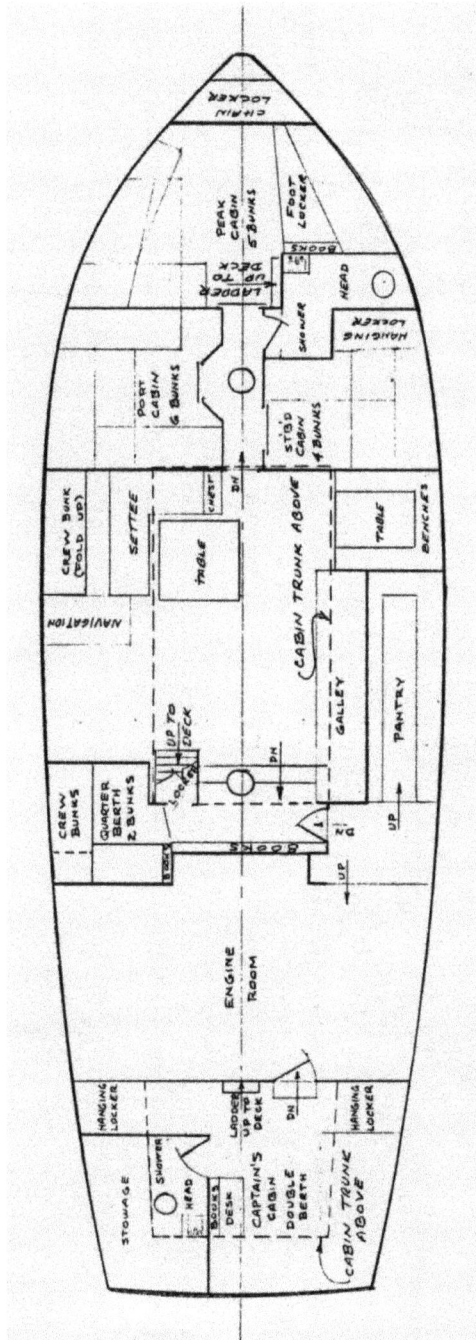

Below deck layout from the Baker's marketing brochure

In 1988 *Anne Kristine* went in for repairs at the D.N. Kelley and Son shipyard in Fairhaven, Massachusetts. The Wichmann engine was removed and replaced with a new Cummins diesel rated at 150 horsepower. The Wichmann was taken by the Coolspring Power Museum with the intent to restore and display it. While *Anne Kristine* was on the railway the naval architect Dan Blachly measured her then drew a lines plan and a sail plan. He also performed an inclining experiment to determine her displacement and center of gravity. With those, he performed a stability analysis to show that she met the requirements for sail training vessels in Canada. The lines plan reveals that the bottom aft was distorted upward. The keel had been filled in to compensate and make the bottom of the keel straight.

The following figure is a lines drawing based on the drawings of Dan Blachly. The drawing was created in the 3-D hull development program Delftship. The shape has been modified to remove the distortion found in the bottom and so approximate what her shape was originally. The hull has been trimmed 3 degrees aft to show a typical loading condition. The keel, stem and stern timber are not shown

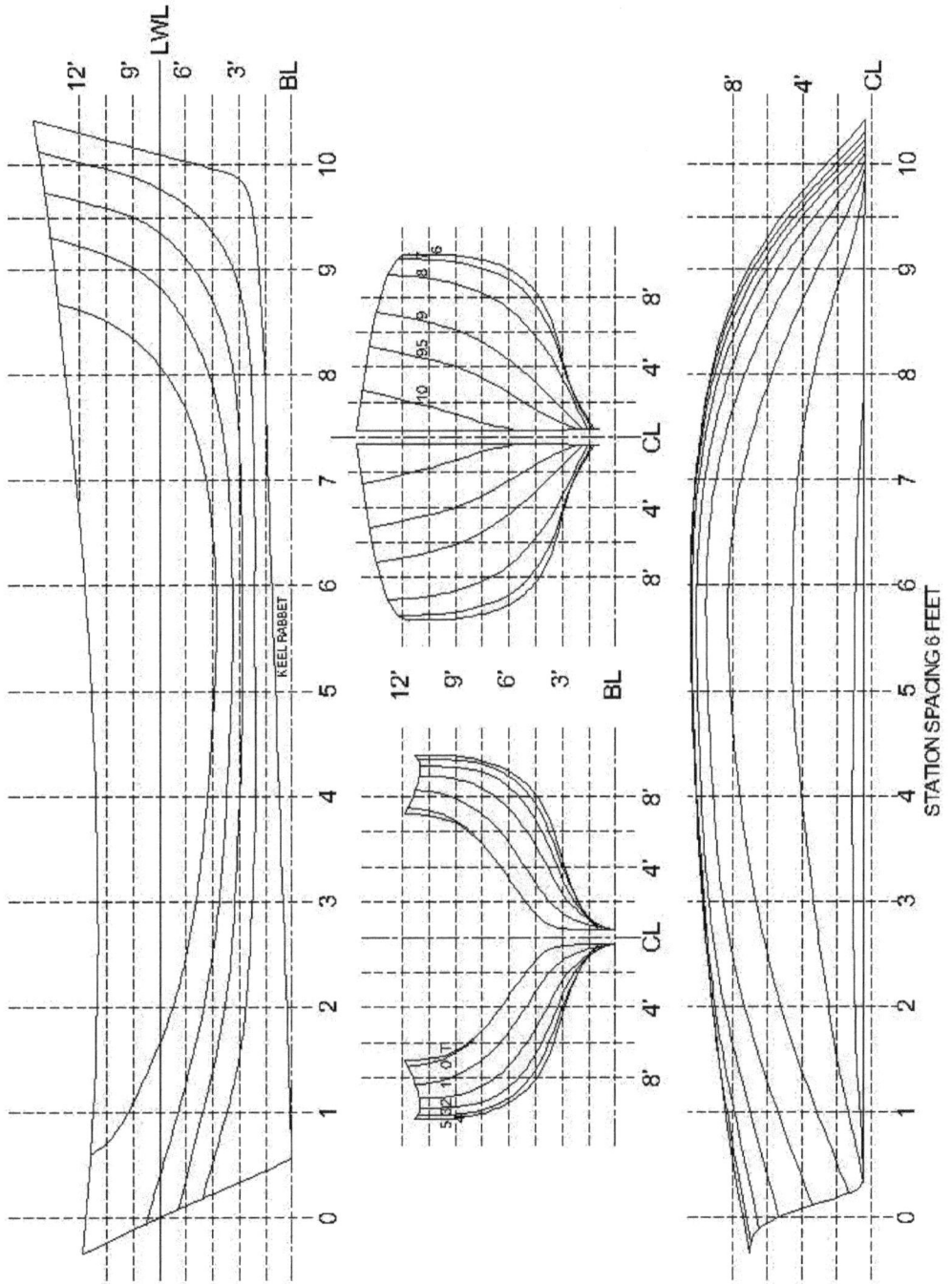

Anne Kristine's last voyage

In the following section time is an important element. The U.S. Coast Guard used Romeo Time in all their reports; that is Zulu or Universal Time minus 5 hours. It corresponds to Eastern Standard Time. However, the East Coast of the U.S. was observing Daylight Savings Time. Time used in this narrative is Eastern Standard Time in 12-hour format.

In 1991, Norman booked the first winter assignments for *Anne Kristine*. One was with Cornell University for a seminar and another was with The Center for Coastal Studies in Provincetown for whale studies off of Tortola and Santo Domingo. The charters would begin January first. *Anne Kristine* was hauled out and put in top condition in preparation for the voyage. Baker needed time to work on a film about *Anne Kristine* so he hired a professional captain, Joey Gelband, to take her first to Bermuda then on to Tortola. Gelband was licensed as a Master and had sailed on *Anne Kristine* and the schooner Ernestina as first mate, but this was his first assignment as captain. Also on board was Peter Abelman who had sailed on every trip that *Anne Kristine* made after she came to New York. Five men and two women made up the rest of the crew; some had sailing experience while for others it was their first voyage. Unfortunately, the insurance company cancelled the policy on the boat before they departed.

On the morning of October 25, a Friday, they started out from Muller Boat Works on Mill Basin in Brooklyn and set a course for Bermuda under power. The departure date was chosen with the thought that it was the end of the hurricane season. When sailing from the U.S. to the Caribbean it is best to cross the Gulf Stream as soon as possible. To go south along the coast could mean fighting a current of up to 2-1/2 knots. Also, the seas can become steep if the wind blows against the current. The course from New York to Bermuda, about 137 degrees true, gets one across the Gulf Stream with the pleasant, mid-ocean refuge of Bermuda as the goal.

71

The next day the wind came up and they set the sails. The weather was fine for *Anne Kristine* and her crew, but to the south of Bermuda a depression had developed into a subtropical storm.

On Sunday, the 27th, the storm was upgraded to a tropical storm and given the name Grace. Gelband altered course to the east in an attempt to avoid the storm thinking it was on a course for the Atlantic Coast. The weather worsened and in late afternoon they shortened sail. At 5:00 pm the National Weather Service reported that Grace was a hurricane with sustained winds of 65 knots and gusts to 80 knots. Grace was still more than 300 nm away from *Anne Kristine* and was moving north. That report and those that followed indicated that 34 knot winds and 12-foot seas could be expected at 350 nm from the hurricane. Grace was never a strong hurricane but had a wide reach.

On Monday, the 28th, the situation deteriorated rapidly. The seas had grown until they were washing over the vessel and she began to take on water. Gelband changed course to the west, running before the wind in an attempt to make Chesapeake Bay. About noon he called the Coast Guard and reported that they were taking on water. Their position was about halfway between New York and Bermuda and they had just crossed the line of their original course. They were also at a point where any port on the East Coast was about the same distance. Delaware Bay was the closest at 275 nm. Chesapeake Bay was 300 nm away. There was no easy way out of their predicament and they were out of reach of rescue helicopters. The Coast Guard diverted a C-130 and the cutter Forward to *Anne Kristine*'s position. Understand that the crew was out in the open facing storm force winds and heavy wind and spray. There was no shelter on deck.

12:55 pm - Gelband called to update their position and course. He reported that they were keeping up with the water and were not in immediate danger. The C-130 located *Anne Kristine* then returned to base at Elizabeth City. The cutter *Forward* was released from the operation.

3:00 pm - He called with a position update and reported winds of 40 to 60 knots and seas of 15 plus feet.

4:00 pm - He called with a position update and reported winds of 65 to 75 knots and seas of 20 to 25 feet. The Coast Guard recommended a westerly course to avoid the path of the hurricane.

4:40 pm - He reported that they had dropped sails and were under power and were keeping up with the water.

5:00 pm - The sun had set and darkness moved in. On paper, the track of hurricane Grace looked like it would continue on to the northwest at a reasonable pace but, at about 5 pm, it stalled in the face of a cold front, changed direction and moved east. High seas had built up because of the center staying in a small area for hours.

6:39 pm - Gelband reported that they were unable to keep up with the water and requested additional pumps and to evacuate the crew. They were about to lose the generator and with it the electric pumps. He intended to put the crew in an 18-man life raft but he would stay on board and try to save the vessel. Wind was from the northeast at 60 knots, seas were 20-25 feet.

There were six pumps on *Anne Kristine*; two DC powered bilge pumps to keep up with normal seepage, two 110-volt pumps with higher capacity powered by the generator, a hand-powered diaphragm pump, and a gasoline engine pump for emergencies. They took the gas-powered pump on deck and with that kept up with the water. They had trouble keeping the pump running because of waves breaking over it. Eventually it quit and wouldn't start again.

7:21 pm - Gelband reported that the freeboard was down to two feet. The freeboard was typically about 3 ½ feet.

7:30 pm - The Coast Guard launched a C-130 from Elizabeth City with de-watering pumps on board. An HH-60 Jayhawk rescue helicopter launched at 8:00 followed by another an hour and a half later. *Anne Kristine* had made progress to the west but was still beyond the Jayhawk's range. A head wind made matters worse for the helicopters. The first Jayhawk out was serial number 6008 commanded by Lieutenant Paul Lange. He knew that *Anne Kristine* was out of range so he asked the dispatcher to find a ship they could use to refuel. The aircraft carrier *USS America* was at sea off of Virginia performing sea trials to test repairs to her boilers[10]. They were in rough seas when they got the call from the Coast Guard requesting assistance. Captain Kent Ewing quickly agreed to assist. He later said "I was riding as rough as I have ever seen on a carrier." The Jayhawks used America as a 'lilypad', refueled and continued to *Anne Kristine*. Lt. Lange had plenty of practice landing on pitching decks from his days as a Marine aviator.

9:32 pm - Gelband reported that their course was between 245 and 270 degrees and that they were making 10-1/2 knots and surfing down the waves.

There is a wave buoy that lays 150 nm from Cape Hatteras. It was somewhat closer than *Anne Kristine* to the hurricane. It measured "significant" wave heights of up to 6.6 meters at this time. According to wave statistics, the highest waves could be estimated to reach 13 meters (42 feet). This is pretty close to what Peter Abelman described as 50-foot waves.

The C-130 reached *Anne Kristine* about 9:50 and tried to drop pumps but none could be retrieved. The first was actually dropped to the wrong ship, a Danish trawler, *Tyborg*. The second missed and on the third try the retrieval line was cut by the propeller. The second Jayhawk had problems with its navigational system so it was decided that the first helicopter would try to rescue everyone. The C-130 stayed on site and provided a communication link and a point for the second helicopter to home in on.

---

[10] *Previously, at the end of August in that year, USS America rescued three shipwrecked yachtsmen, one was a pregnant woman, who had been at sea in a raft for ten days. America then sailed on to participate in a NATO exercise, Northstar 91, in which she operated in the Vestfjord of Norway.

11:03 pm - Gelband reported that the water was gaining and the freeboard was down to 1-1/2 feet. At this point they were about 260 nm east of the entrance to Chesapeake Bay.

The first Jayhawk reached *Anne Kristine* at 11:30. It would be impossible to hoist people from the deck because of the wild motions and the masts and rigging swinging through space. The crew had to jump over one by one as *Anne Kristine* raced away. They went over wearing life jackets and everyone had some form of light. For the first two rescues the rescue swimmer, Duane Jones, was dropped to assist but he was soon exhausted and wasn't dropped again. The remaining crew members managed to climb from the sea into the hoist basket on their own. The helicopter had to hover low and close to the waves then climb frantically to avoid the higher waves as they passed. The Jayhawk was new to Coast Guard service and this was the first instance of a Jayhawk pulling survivors from the sea.

At 12:23, with all onboard, Lieutenant Lange headed back to **USS America**. He caught a final glimpse of *Anne Kristine* as she turned sideways to the waves with no one at the helm to correct her course. On board the carrier the crew of *Anne Kristine* were treated, and got hot showers and blankets before they took off for Elizabeth City.

Gelband had a tough telephone call to make. He had to call Norman Baker to explain what had happened.

The crew of Jayhawk 6008 received an award from the American Helicopter Society for their achievements. Norman Baker sent a telegram to the aircrew which read: "Only through your enormous courage and consummate skill and with the marvelous instrument Sikorsky placed in your hands, was the *Anne Kristine*'s crew rescued that apocalyptic night."

For those caught in it, hurricane Grace was a frightful experience but the weather would get worse in the coming days. The remains of hurricane Grace merged with another storm to create "The Perfect Storm" requiring even more heroics from the Coast Guard and the Air National Guard.

Joey Gelband quit the sea and took up farming.

The same Jayhawk, serial 6008,
shown during a demonstration of sea rescue in Seattle.
Photo by Brandon Weeks via Wikimedia Commons

USS America in the Vestfjord of Norway
with the Lofoten islands in the background.
U.S. Navy photograph

CHART OF THE VOYAGE AND THE TRACK OF GRACE

The following chart is plotted on a hurricane tracking chart which uses equal distances for latitude and longitude. This makes the chart distorted but makes it much easier to plot positions.

The numbers on the tracks show locations approximately at the same times for *Anne Kristine* and Grace. Distinct points are accurate positions. Otherwise, the tracks are conjectural.

Descriptions for the chart

1. Friday morning: A/K departs Jamaica Bay under power on a course for Bermuda.

Friday afternoon: A subtropical depression is identified south of Bermuda.

2. Saturday after midnight: The depression becomes a subtropical storm.

Saturday morning: A/K raises sail in fine weather.

3. Sunday morning: A/K turns east in an attempt to skirt the storm. The storm begins to change course from northeast to northwest

4. Sunday mid-day: The storm is designated a tropical storm named Grace and is moving northwest at 9 knots.

5. Sunday evening: Grace becomes a hurricane

6. Monday after midnight: Grace stalls for at least 6 hours during the night.

7. Monday: At 10 am, A/K changes course to the west. Grace reaches her northernmost position and closest to A/K at about 270 nm.

8: Monday: At noon A/K crosses her original course to Bermuda, 28 hours after she turned east. A/K calls the CG to report they were taking on water. Grace has turned east and picks up speed moving away from A/K.

9. Tuesday after midnight: The crew is rescued. Grace passes south of Bermuda.

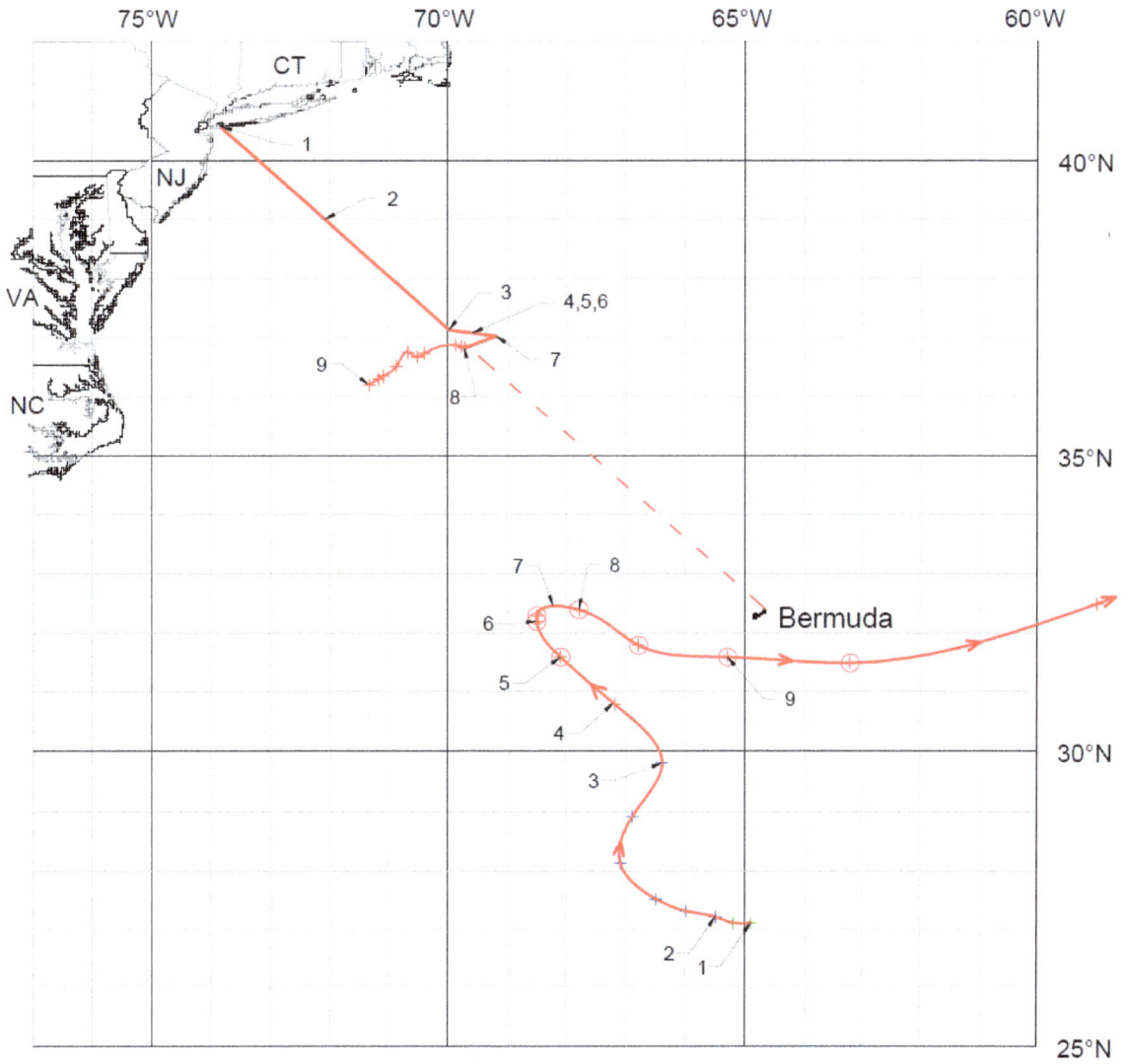

Sources for this chapter:

Video; Anne Kristine by Norman and Mary Ann Baker

News & Record; Greensboro, N.C.; A series of four articles by Donald W. Patterson:

Rescue to Remember | Posted: Saturday, September 5, 1992

Sailing Toward Harm's Way | Posted: Sunday, September 6, 1992

Night of Miracles | Posted: Saturday, September 7, 1992

Snatched from the Waves | Posted: Saturday, September 8, 1992

At the helm of USS America: the aircraft carrier and its 23 commanders, 1965-1996; James U. Wise, Jr., and Scott Baron; 2014

USCG records including situation reports, summary reports and press releases provided by the Historian's Office.

National Hurricane Center (NOAA) - online archives - http://www.nhc.noaa.gov/archive/storm_wallets/atlantic/

EPILOG

Anne Kristine lies at the bottom of the ocean in 13,500 feet of water while the Wichmann engine is well cared for at Mystic Seaport. *Gjøa* is now restored and is displayed in a special hall at the Norwegian Maritime Museum.

Tolleif Hidle was working on research for this story when he became seriously ill and passed away in 2017. Norman Baker died in 2017 at the age of 89 when his private plane crashed in bad weather. His wife Mary Ann had died earlier from cancer. As of early 2021, the Sauholmen brothers were alive and well in Norway and Einar was still repairing boats. Göran Grauers was in retirement in Sweden.

APPENDIX: THE ENGINES

In 1936, it appeared that **Stine Katrine** had ended her days as a sailing vessel for that is when Andreas Fenstad bought her and put in an engine. Over the next 55 years she had five different engines that we know about. Three of them were used engines, a sign of frugal owners. After she was sailing again, the engines were still important for maneuvering and to drive her through calms.

Sindre Nilsen found and shared the Norwegian government record showing basic information for the first four engines. Included in the record is the manufacturer's name and the official horsepower as determined by a simple formula. This power is what appears in the official registers and is usually lower than the manufacturer's stated power.

Three of the engines were semi-diesels. While a true diesel uses very high compression (500 psi) to ignite the fuel, a semi-diesel works at much lower compression (185 psi) but requires a red-hot element to ignite the fuel. Semi-diesels typically used the action of the pistons to pump scavenging air through the crankcase and into the cylinders.

The model of each engine was not in the record so to arrive at an educated guess as to what model was installed, a comparison was made between the listed official horsepower and a horsepower calculated from data for different engine models.

Formula for two-stroke semi-diesels: $$HK = \frac{d^2 \ \sqrt[3]{s} \ n}{12600}$$

Formula for two-stroke diesels: $$HK = \frac{d^2 \ \sqrt[3]{s} \ n}{8400}$$

HK = hestekrefter = horsepower
d = piston diameter, millimeters
s = stroke, millimeters
n = number of cylinders

The fifth engine was a modern Cummins diesel installed in the US.

Engine no. 1

The first engine was a used one-cylinder June-Munktell semi-diesel which came from the cutter *Pilot*.

Model: June-Munktell 40 M or 40 MV

Built: 1931, Jönköpings Motorfabrik, Jönköping, Sweden

Installed in Åsta 1:   1936

Horsepower: 40

RPM: 400

Number of cylinders: 1

Bore and Stroke: 260 x 310 mm

Calculated HP: 36.3

Official HP: 36

Engine no. 2

The second engine was a two-cylinder Deutz full diesel and appears to have been a model SOMZ 130. It may have been new but at least wasn't very old. S=ship motor; O=two-stroke diesel; M=water-cooled; Z=two cylinder; 1=first variant; 30=30 cm stroke.

Deutz OM diesels had a distinctive feature in that scavenging air was pumped in by large diameter pistons on the side of the engine.

The previous engine must have been inadequate at only 40 HP so the Deutz at 70 HP was likely a necessary upgrade. It could have been installed any time after 1936, perhaps when *Åsta 1* was repaired after it sank in 1944 at Kristiansund.

Model: Deutz SOMZ 130

Built: circa 1938, Klöckner-Humboldt-Deutz AG, Cologne, Germany.

Installed in Åsta 1:   1944 or earlier

Horsepower: 70

RPM: 450

Number of cylinders: 2

Bore and Stroke: 200 x 300 mm

Calculated HP: 63.7

Official HP: 63

William Knudsen was an importer of Deutz engines. Ads like this ran from 1937 into 1945.

The engine in the ad is an SOMZ 117 or 122, smaller than the SOMZ 130.

An ad for a shipyard in Kristiansund. They were an agent for Deutz and this may be where *Åsta 1* got her new engine.

A Deutz SOMZ 130 from 1938 in the Dutch tugboat *De Vliet*.
Photo courtesy of Berdie de Ruiter

A Deutz SOMZ 130 where the muffler and the scavenging pump have been cut open. The piston of the scavenging pump is visible. The clutch and reverse gear are not in place.

Photo taken at the Scheepvaartmuseum, Duisburg, Netherlands. Courtesy of Pieter Klein

Engine no. 3

The third engine was another used June-Munktell semi-diesel but much larger at 120 hp. It was installed when *Åsta 1* was owned by Ramsvik and Eidsaune.

Model: June-Munktell MV 602
Built: 1938, Jönköpings Motorfabrik, Jönköping, Sweden
Installed in *Åsta 1*:   1951
Horsepower: 120
RPM: 325
Number of cylinders: 2
Bore and Stroke: 310 x 380 mm
Calculated HP: 110.5
Official HP: 111
Weight: about 7000 kg., 15,000 pounds

Typical two-cylinder June-Munktell of the period.

Engine no. 4

The fourth engine was a Wichmann semi-diesel, Type 2AB. Wichmann engines were built on the island of Bømlo at Rubbestadneset, a town which was on the steamship route south from Bergen. Today the trip can be made in an hour and a half by fast passenger ferry.

Built as Type 2A: 1941
    by M. Haldorsen & Sønners Motorfabrikk, Rubbestadneset, Norway
Rebuilt as Type 2AB: 1947
Motor number: 3400
Installed in ***Anne Kristine***: 1963
Horsepower: 120
RPM: 350
Number of cylinders: 2
Bore and Stroke: 320 x 320 mm
Calculated HP: 111.2
Official HP: 111
Propeller: Two blades, 1.2-meter diameter, adjustable, reversible
Weight: 5000 kg, 11,000 pounds

This is the engine we know most about since the engine is preserved at Mystic Seaport and the Wichmann records have been preserved by a volunteer group in Norway. Even with these records, identification was a challenge since the builder's plate had been removed. This engine has an unusual history. Wichmann was a respected builder of semi-diesel engines and they eventually developed full diesels. Their Type A diesel came out in 1937 with 50 horsepower per cylinder. Our engine was originally built as a Type A, two-cylinder engine in 1941 during the German occupation as shown below.

A Type 2A Wichmann diesel with 100 horsepower
Note that the cylinders are square in cross-section.

After the war, Wichmann produced a semi-diesel, Type AB, which used the same base and crankshaft as the Type A. It was rated at 60 HP per cylinder. Type A engines could be converted to a Type AB and vice versa by changing the pistons and cylinders. Our engine was converted from a Type A to a Type AB in 1947.

The Type AB engines had electric glow plugs so it wasn't necessary to use a blow torch to start them. They were supplied with adjustable pitch propellers which, in the case of *Anne Kristine's* engine, was controlled by a hand crank in the pilothouse. Hydraulic propeller control was an option on the 2AB. There was a clutch but no gears and the adjustable propeller was used to reverse the thrust. The propeller was two-bladed with a diameter of 1.2 meters.

The engine was originally installed to replace a steam engine in the *Busta* in 1941 when she was converted from a whale catcher to a freight boat. In 1958 she got a new owner and a new name, *Katland*. Less than a year later, in August of 1959, she ran aground and sank in 100 feet of water off the southern coast of Norway. After a month of work, she was raised and the bottom repaired.

In 1962 *Katland* was offered for sale in a wrecked condition but it appears that the machinery had been preserved. She was bought by Berge Saw and Lumber Company (known as Berge Bruk) which also had a shipyard. They in turn offered the engine for sale. *Katland,* built of steel, was cut up for scrap.

**FRAKTEFARTØYET
-KATLAND-**
til salgs i havarert stand. Tidligere hvalbåt, bygget av stål 1910, ombygget 1941. 108 tonn br. 150 tonn dw. 120 HK Wichmann A.B. 8 HK Armstrong hjelpemotor, 12 HK Lidan dekksvinsj. Gode seil, stor luke 7x2,5 m og ellers vanlig utstyr. Motor og annet utstyr kan eventuelt selges hver for seg. — Henvendelse O. Westmoen, Farsund, tlf. 495 etter kl. 18.

An ad which appeared in the periodical <u>Fiskaren</u> on October 10, 1962 offering the *Katland* and her machinery for sale.

TIL SALGS
100—120 HK Wichmann type AB. Byggeår 1941, ombygget i 1947 i godkjent stand, selges rimelig
Berge sag og trelastforretning,
Telefon 110, Ølen — Ølensvaag.

An ad which appeared in the periodical <u>Fiskaren</u> on November 21, 1962 offering the Wichmann engine for sale.

When the Hidle family bought *Åsta 1* (soon to be *Anne Kristine*), the June-Munktell engine was 13 years old and by 1962 it was 24 years old. The offered Wichmann 2AB was just 15 years old. The factory where it was built was a short distance away on the same island and a lot of Wichmann competence was available. Hans Hidle decided to buy it and took out a loan of 15,000 kroner.

94

Anne Kristine was based on the east side of Bømlo island and Berge Bruk was in Ølensvåg, both off of the Hardangerfjord, a trip of about 30 nautical miles. It seems likely that *Anne Kristine* was taken to Berge Bruk to have the engine dropped in. The Wichmann remained in *Anne Kristine* for another 25 years but became a problem for later owners. Finally, in 1988, it was replaced with a new Cummins diesel at the D.N. Kelley & Son shipyard in Fairhaven, MA. The Wichmann was given to the Coolspring Power Museum in Pennsylvania, but after further consideration by Coolspring, the engine went to Mystic Seaport in 1992. Volunteers at Mystic devoted 3,300 hours over two years to dismantle and restore the engine. Many parts had to be recreated based on the original worn parts. It is now on display and is run regularly.

Loaded on the truck for the trip to the Coolspring Power Museum.
Photo courtesy of the Museum

The Wichmann 2AB on display at Mystic Seaport in 2011.
Photo by the Author.

The Wichmann 2AB on display at Mystic Seaport in 2011.
Photo by the Author.

Engine no. 5

The fifth engine was a Cummins 4-stroke, high-speed, diesel. It was naturally aspirated and not turbocharged as are most engines in this family. It operated at much higher rpm than the previously installed engines. Even with a reduction gear with a deep ratio the propeller speed would be too high for the four-foot diameter propeller that came with the Wichmann. Also, the controls for the propeller were part of the Wichmann engine that was removed. Details of the new reduction gear and propeller were not found. The model of the engine had to be worked out by examining blurred movie footage taken in the engine room.

Model: C Series, 6C8.3
Built: 1988, Cummins Engine Co., Inc., Columbus, Indiana
Installed: 1988
Horsepower: 155
RPM: 2500
Number of cylinders: 6
Bore and Stroke: 114 x 135 mm
Displacement: 8.27 liters
Weight of engine: 692 kg, 1525 pounds
Weight of reduction gear
      assuming 5:1 ratio: 300 kg, 660 pounds

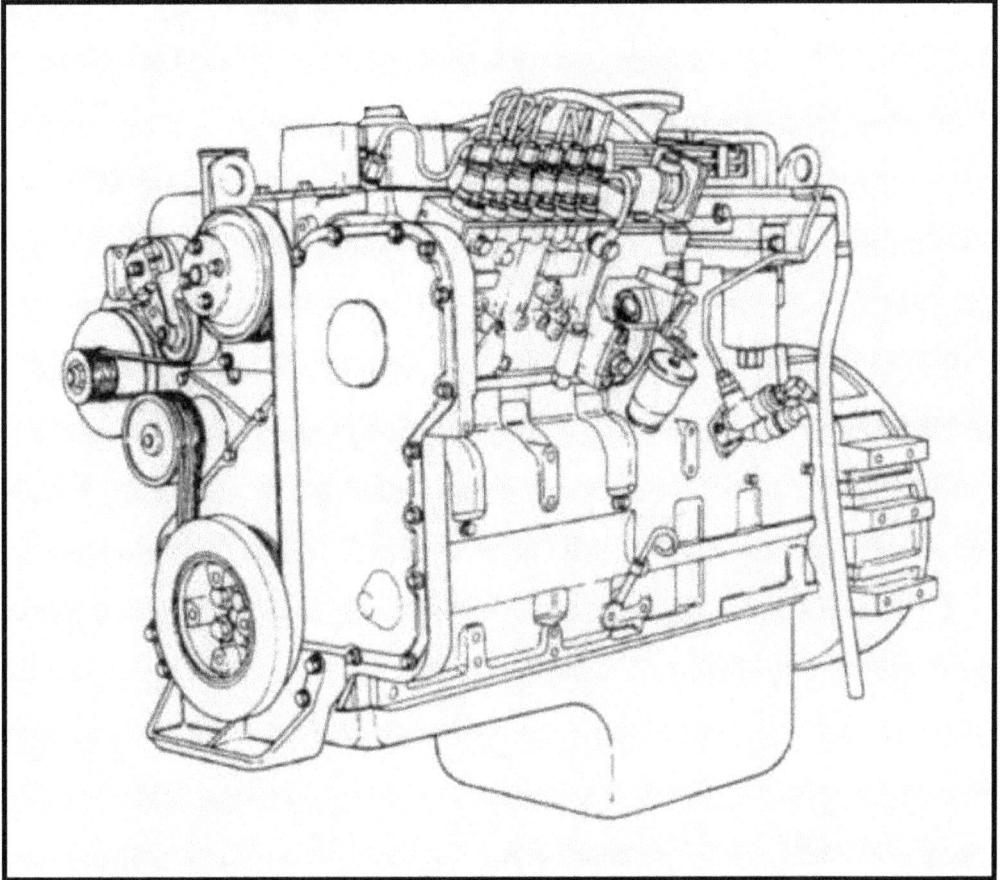

The basic Cummins C-Series 8.3-liter engine

References

Adolph Berg; Bergen i gamle dage; 1925

Toril Grande, Anders Slembe; "Anna Kristine", "Dyrafjeld" - Én jakt, to navn, mange liv!

Torbjørn Hertel-Aas; Jekter og Jektefart; Stavanger Sjøfartsmuseet; 1990

Tolleif Hidle; Treet vårt, Minne frå barndom og oppvekst på Hidlegarden; 2016

Olav Kolltveit, Jondal i gamal og ny tid; J.D Beyer; 1953

Christian, Koren-Wiberg; Det tyske kontor i Bergen; 1899

Bernt Lorentzen; Handelshuset Herman von Tangens sønner AS; 1946

Lars Melkersson; Svenske Fiskebåtsmotorer, Del 3; 2010

Hans Nerhus; Frå Vikings Tid Til Vår Tid; 1955

Halldor Opedal; Hardingar på sjøen; Norsk Bokreidingslag; 1995

Kristoffer Rein; Stadsbygd, Bind II; Trondheim, 1999

W.M. Schjelderup; Katalog over Bergens Skipperforenings Samling, 1917

Valdemar Steiro; Gammelmotoren; 1991

Malvin Toft; Båtar med sjel; Førde; 2002

Toralf Tvedt; Bjoa og Nordlandsfarten; Sunnhordland Årbok, Band XLV; 1964

Wilhelm Ulrich; Schiffsdieselmachinen; 1942

Bård Gram Økland, Per Kristian Sebak, Tore L. Nilsen; Maritime Bergen; 2014

www.ingramcontent.com/pod-product-compliance
Lightning Source LLC
Chambersburg PA
CBHW040254100426
42811CB00011B/1263